🎼 PERFOR/

DATE _____ LOCATION _____

ACCOMPANIST _____

_____   _____

MW01537685

SONGS PERFORMED

	PERSONAL RATING
_____	☆ ☆ ☆ ☆ ☆
_____	☆ ☆ ☆ ☆ ☆
_____	☆ ☆ ☆ ☆ ☆
_____	☆ ☆ ☆ ☆ ☆
_____	☆ ☆ ☆ ☆ ☆

ACCOMPANIST/PERFORMED WITH NOTES

OVERALL THOUGHTS

Ratings ☆ ☆ ☆ ☆ ☆

🎼 PERFORMANCE LOG

DATE _____ LOCATION _____

ACCOMPANIST _____ PERFORMED WITH _____

_____   _____

SONGS PERFORMED	PERSONAL RATING
	☆ ☆ ☆ ☆ ☆
	☆ ☆ ☆ ☆ ☆
	☆ ☆ ☆ ☆ ☆
	☆ ☆ ☆ ☆ ☆
	☆ ☆ ☆ ☆ ☆

ACCOMPANIST/PERFORMED WITH NOTES

OVERALL THOUGHTS

Ratings ☆ ☆ ☆ ☆ ☆

♪ PERFORMANCE LOG

DATE _____ LOCATION _____

ACCOMPANIST _____ PERFORMED WITH _____

_____ _____

SONGS PERFORMED   PERSONAL RATING

_____	☆ ☆ ☆ ☆ ☆
_____	☆ ☆ ☆ ☆ ☆
_____	☆ ☆ ☆ ☆ ☆
_____	☆ ☆ ☆ ☆ ☆
_____	☆ ☆ ☆ ☆ ☆

ACCOMPANIST/PERFORMED WITH NOTES

OVERALL THOUGHTS

Ratings ☆ ☆ ☆ ☆ ☆

𝄞 PERFORMANCE LOG

DATE _____ LOCATION _____

ACCOMPANIST _____ PERFORMED WITH _____

_____ _____

SONGS PERFORMED   PERSONAL RATING

	☆ ☆ ☆ ☆ ☆
	☆ ☆ ☆ ☆ ☆
	☆ ☆ ☆ ☆ ☆
	☆ ☆ ☆ ☆ ☆
	☆ ☆ ☆ ☆ ☆

ACCOMPANIST/PERFORMED WITH NOTES

OVERALL THOUGHTS

Ratings ☆ ☆ ☆ ☆ ☆

𝄞 PERFORMANCE LOG

DATE _____ LOCATION _____

ACCOMPANIST _____ PERFORMED WITH _____

_____   _____

SONGS PERFORMED   PERSONAL RATING

_____	☆ ☆ ☆ ☆ ☆
_____	☆ ☆ ☆ ☆ ☆
_____	☆ ☆ ☆ ☆ ☆
_____	☆ ☆ ☆ ☆ ☆
_____	☆ ☆ ☆ ☆ ☆

ACCOMPANIST/PERFORMED WITH NOTES

OVERALL THOUGHTS

Ratings ☆ ☆ ☆ ☆ ☆

𝄞 PERFORMANCE LOG

DATE _____ LOCATION _____

ACCOMPANIST _____ PERFORMED WITH _____

_____   _____

SONGS PERFORMED   PERSONAL RATING

	☆ ☆ ☆ ☆ ☆
	☆ ☆ ☆ ☆ ☆
	☆ ☆ ☆ ☆ ☆
	☆ ☆ ☆ ☆ ☆
	☆ ☆ ☆ ☆ ☆

ACCOMPANIST/PERFORMED WITH NOTES

OVERALL THOUGHTS

Ratings ☆ ☆ ☆ ☆ ☆

♪ PERFORMANCE LOG

DATE _____ LOCATION _____

ACCOMPANIST _____ PERFORMED WITH _____

_____ _____

SONGS PERFORMED

Song	PERSONAL RATING
	☆ ☆ ☆ ☆ ☆
	☆ ☆ ☆ ☆ ☆
	☆ ☆ ☆ ☆ ☆
	☆ ☆ ☆ ☆ ☆
	☆ ☆ ☆ ☆ ☆

ACCOMPANIST/PERFORMED WITH NOTES

OVERALL THOUGHTS

Ratings ☆ ☆ ☆ ☆ ☆

♪ PERFORMANCE LOG

DATE _____ LOCATION _____

ACCOMPANIST _____ PERFORMED WITH _____

_____   _____

SONGS PERFORMED   PERSONAL RATING

	☆ ☆ ☆ ☆ ☆
	☆ ☆ ☆ ☆ ☆
	☆ ☆ ☆ ☆ ☆
	☆ ☆ ☆ ☆ ☆
	☆ ☆ ☆ ☆ ☆

ACCOMPANIST/PERFORMED WITH NOTES

OVERALL THOUGHTS

Ratings ☆ ☆ ☆ ☆ ☆

♪ PERFORMANCE LOG

DATE _____ LOCATION _____

ACCOMPANIST _____ PERFORMED WITH _____

_____ _____

SONGS PERFORMED

PERSONAL RATING

Song	Rating
_____	☆ ☆ ☆ ☆ ☆
_____	☆ ☆ ☆ ☆ ☆
_____	☆ ☆ ☆ ☆ ☆
_____	☆ ☆ ☆ ☆ ☆
_____	☆ ☆ ☆ ☆ ☆

ACCOMPANIST / PERFORMED WITH NOTES

OVERALL THOUGHTS

Ratings ☆ ☆ ☆ ☆ ☆

🎼 PERFORMANCE LOG

DATE _____ LOCATION _____

ACCOMPANIST _____ PERFORMED WITH _____

_____ _____

SONGS PERFORMED   PERSONAL RATING

Songs Performed	Personal Rating
	☆ ☆ ☆ ☆ ☆
	☆ ☆ ☆ ☆ ☆
	☆ ☆ ☆ ☆ ☆
	☆ ☆ ☆ ☆ ☆
	☆ ☆ ☆ ☆ ☆

ACCOMPANIST/PERFORMED WITH NOTES

OVERALL THOUGHTS

Ratings ☆ ☆ ☆ ☆ ☆

𝄞 PERFORMANCE LOG

DATE _____ LOCATION _____

ACCOMPANIST _____ PERFORMED WITH _____

_____ _____

SONGS PERFORMED   PERSONAL RATING

_____ ☆ ☆ ☆ ☆ ☆
_____ ☆ ☆ ☆ ☆ ☆
_____ ☆ ☆ ☆ ☆ ☆
_____ ☆ ☆ ☆ ☆ ☆
_____ ☆ ☆ ☆ ☆ ☆

ACCOMPANIST/PERFORMED WITH NOTES

OVERALL THOUGHTS

Ratings ☆ ☆ ☆ ☆ ☆

𝄞 PERFORMANCE LOG

DATE _____ LOCATION _____

ACCOMPANIST _____ PERFORMED WITH _____

_____ _____

SONGS PERFORMED	PERSONAL RATING
	☆ ☆ ☆ ☆ ☆
	☆ ☆ ☆ ☆ ☆
	☆ ☆ ☆ ☆ ☆
	☆ ☆ ☆ ☆ ☆
	☆ ☆ ☆ ☆ ☆

ACCOMPANIST/PERFORMED WITH NOTES

OVERALL THOUGHTS

Ratings ☆ ☆ ☆ ☆ ☆

♪ PERFORMANCE LOG

DATE _____ LOCATION _____

ACCOMPANIST _____ PERFORMED WITH _____

_____   _____

SONGS PERFORMED   PERSONAL RATING

Song	Rating
_____	☆ ☆ ☆ ☆ ☆
_____	☆ ☆ ☆ ☆ ☆
_____	☆ ☆ ☆ ☆ ☆
_____	☆ ☆ ☆ ☆ ☆
_____	☆ ☆ ☆ ☆ ☆

ACCOMPANIST/PERFORMED WITH NOTES

OVERALL THOUGHTS

Ratings ☆ ☆ ☆ ☆ ☆

𝄞 PERFORMANCE LOG

DATE _____ LOCATION _____

ACCOMPANIST _____ PERFORMED WITH _____

_____   _____

SONGS PERFORMED   PERSONAL RATING

	☆ ☆ ☆ ☆ ☆
	☆ ☆ ☆ ☆ ☆
	☆ ☆ ☆ ☆ ☆
	☆ ☆ ☆ ☆ ☆
	☆ ☆ ☆ ☆ ☆

ACCOMPANIST/PERFORMED WITH NOTES

OVERALL THOUGHTS

Ratings ☆ ☆ ☆ ☆ ☆

🎼 PERFORMANCE LOG

Date _____ Location _____

Accompanist _____ Performed with _____

_____ _____

Songs Performed

Personal Rating

Songs	☆ ☆ ☆ ☆ ☆
	☆ ☆ ☆ ☆ ☆
	☆ ☆ ☆ ☆ ☆
	☆ ☆ ☆ ☆ ☆
	☆ ☆ ☆ ☆ ☆

Accompanist/Performed with Notes

Overall Thoughts

Ratings ☆ ☆ ☆ ☆ ☆

𝄞 PERFORMANCE LOG

DATE _____ LOCATION _____

ACCOMPANIST _____ PERFORMED WITH _____

_____ _____

SONGS PERFORMED

	PERSONAL RATING
	☆ ☆ ☆ ☆ ☆
	☆ ☆ ☆ ☆ ☆
	☆ ☆ ☆ ☆ ☆
	☆ ☆ ☆ ☆ ☆
	☆ ☆ ☆ ☆ ☆

ACCOMPANIST/PERFORMED WITH NOTES

OVERALL THOUGHTS

Ratings ☆ ☆ ☆ ☆ ☆

𝄞 PERFORMANCE LOG

DATE _____ LOCATION _____

ACCOMPANIST _____ PERFORMED WITH _____

_____ _____

SONGS PERFORMED   PERSONAL RATING

_____	☆ ☆ ☆ ☆ ☆
_____	☆ ☆ ☆ ☆ ☆
_____	☆ ☆ ☆ ☆ ☆
_____	☆ ☆ ☆ ☆ ☆
_____	☆ ☆ ☆ ☆ ☆

ACCOMPANIST/PERFORMED WITH NOTES

OVERALL THOUGHTS

Ratings ☆ ☆ ☆ ☆ ☆

𝄞 PERFORMANCE LOG

DATE _____ LOCATION _____

ACCOMPANIST _____ PERFORMED WITH _____

_____ _____

SONGS PERFORMED   PERSONAL RATING

	☆ ☆ ☆ ☆ ☆
	☆ ☆ ☆ ☆ ☆
	☆ ☆ ☆ ☆ ☆
	☆ ☆ ☆ ☆ ☆
	☆ ☆ ☆ ☆ ☆

ACCOMPANIST/PERFORMED WITH NOTES

OVERALL THOUGHTS

Ratings ☆ ☆ ☆ ☆ ☆

♪ PERFORMANCE LOG

DATE _____ LOCATION _____

ACCOMPANIST _____ PERFORMED WITH _____

_____ _____

SONGS PERFORMED   PERSONAL RATING

Song	☆ ☆ ☆ ☆ ☆
	☆ ☆ ☆ ☆ ☆
	☆ ☆ ☆ ☆ ☆
	☆ ☆ ☆ ☆ ☆
	☆ ☆ ☆ ☆ ☆
	☆ ☆ ☆ ☆ ☆

ACCOMPANIST/PERFORMED WITH NOTES

OVERALL THOUGHTS

Ratings ☆ ☆ ☆ ☆ ☆

♪ PERFORMANCE LOG

DATE _____ LOCATION _____

ACCOMPANIST _____ PERFORMED WITH _____

_____   _____

SONGS PERFORMED	PERSONAL RATING
	☆ ☆ ☆ ☆ ☆
	☆ ☆ ☆ ☆ ☆
	☆ ☆ ☆ ☆ ☆
	☆ ☆ ☆ ☆ ☆
	☆ ☆ ☆ ☆ ☆

ACCOMPANIST/PERFORMED WITH NOTES

OVERALL THOUGHTS

Ratings ☆ ☆ ☆ ☆ ☆

𝄞 PERFORMANCE LOG

DATE _____ LOCATION _____

ACCOMPANIST _____ PERFORMED WITH _____

_____ _____

SONGS PERFORMED

Songs Performed	Personal Rating
	☆ ☆ ☆ ☆ ☆
	☆ ☆ ☆ ☆ ☆
	☆ ☆ ☆ ☆ ☆
	☆ ☆ ☆ ☆ ☆
	☆ ☆ ☆ ☆ ☆

ACCOMPANIST/PERFORMED WITH NOTES

OVERALL THOUGHTS

Ratings ☆ ☆ ☆ ☆ ☆

🎼 PERFORMANCE LOG

DATE _____ LOCATION _____

ACCOMPANIST _____ PERFORMED WITH _____

_____ _____

SONGS PERFORMED   PERSONAL RATING

	☆ ☆ ☆ ☆ ☆
	☆ ☆ ☆ ☆ ☆
	☆ ☆ ☆ ☆ ☆
	☆ ☆ ☆ ☆ ☆
	☆ ☆ ☆ ☆ ☆

ACCOMPANIST/PERFORMED WITH NOTES

OVERALL THOUGHTS

Ratings ☆ ☆ ☆ ☆ ☆

𝄞 PERFORMANCE LOG

DATE _____ LOCATION _____

ACCOMPANIST _____ PERFORMED WITH _____

_____ _____

SONGS PERFORMED

PERSONAL RATING

_____	☆ ☆ ☆ ☆ ☆
_____	☆ ☆ ☆ ☆ ☆
_____	☆ ☆ ☆ ☆ ☆
_____	☆ ☆ ☆ ☆ ☆
_____	☆ ☆ ☆ ☆ ☆

ACCOMPANIST/PERFORMED WITH NOTES

OVERALL THOUGHTS

Ratings ☆ ☆ ☆ ☆ ☆

🎼 PERFORMANCE LOG

DATE _____ LOCATION _____

ACCOMPANIST _____ PERFORMED WITH _____

_____ _____

SONGS PERFORMED | PERSONAL RATING

Songs Performed	Personal Rating
	☆ ☆ ☆ ☆ ☆
	☆ ☆ ☆ ☆ ☆
	☆ ☆ ☆ ☆ ☆
	☆ ☆ ☆ ☆ ☆
	☆ ☆ ☆ ☆ ☆

ACCOMPANIST/PERFORMED WITH NOTES

OVERALL THOUGHTS

Ratings ☆ ☆ ☆ ☆ ☆

🎼 PERFORMANCE LOG

DATE _____ LOCATION _____

ACCOMPANIST _____ PERFORMED WITH _____

_____ _____

SONGS PERFORMED

	PERSONAL RATING
_____	☆ ☆ ☆ ☆ ☆
_____	☆ ☆ ☆ ☆ ☆
_____	☆ ☆ ☆ ☆ ☆
_____	☆ ☆ ☆ ☆ ☆
_____	☆ ☆ ☆ ☆ ☆

ACCOMPANIST/PERFORMED WITH NOTES

OVERALL THOUGHTS

Ratings ☆ ☆ ☆ ☆ ☆

♪ PERFORMANCE LOG

DATE _____ LOCATION _____

ACCOMPANIST _____ PERFORMED WITH _____

_____   _____

SONGS PERFORMED   PERSONAL RATING

	☆ ☆ ☆ ☆ ☆
	☆ ☆ ☆ ☆ ☆
	☆ ☆ ☆ ☆ ☆
	☆ ☆ ☆ ☆ ☆
	☆ ☆ ☆ ☆ ☆

ACCOMPANIST/PERFORMED WITH NOTES

OVERALL THOUGHTS

Ratings ☆ ☆ ☆ ☆ ☆

♪ PERFORMANCE LOG

DATE _____ LOCATION _____

ACCOMPANIST _____ PERFORMED WITH _____

_____ _____

SONGS PERFORMED	PERSONAL RATING
	☆ ☆ ☆ ☆ ☆
	☆ ☆ ☆ ☆ ☆
	☆ ☆ ☆ ☆ ☆
	☆ ☆ ☆ ☆ ☆
	☆ ☆ ☆ ☆ ☆

ACCOMPANIST/PERFORMED WITH NOTES

OVERALL THOUGHTS

Ratings ☆ ☆ ☆ ☆ ☆

🎼 PERFORMANCE LOG

DATE _____ LOCATION _____

ACCOMPANIST _____ PERFORMED WITH _____

_____   _____

SONGS PERFORMED	PERSONAL RATING
	☆ ☆ ☆ ☆ ☆
	☆ ☆ ☆ ☆ ☆
	☆ ☆ ☆ ☆ ☆
	☆ ☆ ☆ ☆ ☆
	☆ ☆ ☆ ☆ ☆

ACCOMPANIST/PERFORMED WITH NOTES

OVERALL THOUGHTS

Ratings ☆ ☆ ☆ ☆ ☆

🎼 PERFORMANCE LOG

DATE _____ LOCATION _____

ACCOMPANIST _____ PERFORMED WITH _____

_____ _____

SONGS PERFORMED

PERSONAL RATING

☆ ☆ ☆ ☆ ☆

☆ ☆ ☆ ☆ ☆

☆ ☆ ☆ ☆ ☆

☆ ☆ ☆ ☆ ☆

☆ ☆ ☆ ☆ ☆

ACCOMPANIST/PERFORMED WITH NOTES

OVERALL THOUGHTS

Ratings ☆ ☆ ☆ ☆ ☆

𝄞 PERFORMANCE LOG

DATE _____ LOCATION _____

ACCOMPANIST _____ PERFORMED WITH _____

_____ _____

SONGS PERFORMED   PERSONAL RATING

	☆ ☆ ☆ ☆ ☆
	☆ ☆ ☆ ☆ ☆
	☆ ☆ ☆ ☆ ☆
	☆ ☆ ☆ ☆ ☆
	☆ ☆ ☆ ☆ ☆

ACCOMPANIST/PERFORMED WITH NOTES

OVERALL THOUGHTS

Ratings ☆ ☆ ☆ ☆ ☆

𝄞 PERFORMANCE LOG

DATE _____ LOCATION _____

ACCOMPANIST _____ PERFORMED WITH _____

_____   _____

SONGS PERFORMED   PERSONAL RATING

_____   ☆ ☆ ☆ ☆ ☆

_____   ☆ ☆ ☆ ☆ ☆

_____   ☆ ☆ ☆ ☆ ☆

_____   ☆ ☆ ☆ ☆ ☆

_____   ☆ ☆ ☆ ☆ ☆

ACCOMPANIST/PERFORMED WITH NOTES

OVERALL THOUGHTS

Ratings ☆ ☆ ☆ ☆ ☆

𝄞 PERFORMANCE LOG

DATE _____ LOCATION _____

ACCOMPANIST _____ PERFORMED WITH _____

_____ _____

SONGS PERFORMED   PERSONAL RATING

Songs Performed	Personal Rating
	☆ ☆ ☆ ☆ ☆
	☆ ☆ ☆ ☆ ☆
	☆ ☆ ☆ ☆ ☆
	☆ ☆ ☆ ☆ ☆
	☆ ☆ ☆ ☆ ☆

ACCOMPANIST/PERFORMED WITH NOTES

OVERALL THOUGHTS

Ratings ☆ ☆ ☆ ☆ ☆

🎼 PERFORMANCE LOG

DATE _____ LOCATION _____

ACCOMPANIST _____ PERFORMED WITH _____

_____ _____

SONGS PERFORMED

PERSONAL RATING

_____	☆ ☆ ☆ ☆ ☆
_____	☆ ☆ ☆ ☆ ☆
_____	☆ ☆ ☆ ☆ ☆
_____	☆ ☆ ☆ ☆ ☆
_____	☆ ☆ ☆ ☆ ☆

ACCOMPANIST/PERFORMED WITH NOTES

OVERALL THOUGHTS

Ratings ☆ ☆ ☆ ☆ ☆

♪ PERFORMANCE LOG

DATE _____ LOCATION _____

ACCOMPANIST _____ PERFORMED WITH _____

_____ _____

SONGS PERFORMED   PERSONAL RATING

Song	Rating
	☆ ☆ ☆ ☆ ☆
	☆ ☆ ☆ ☆ ☆
	☆ ☆ ☆ ☆ ☆
	☆ ☆ ☆ ☆ ☆
	☆ ☆ ☆ ☆ ☆

ACCOMPANIST/PERFORMED WITH NOTES

OVERALL THOUGHTS

Ratings ☆ ☆ ☆ ☆ ☆

🎼 PERFORMANCE LOG

DATE _____ LOCATION _____

ACCOMPANIST _____ PERFORMED WITH _____

_____   _____

SONGS PERFORMED   PERSONAL RATING

_____	☆ ☆ ☆ ☆ ☆
_____	☆ ☆ ☆ ☆ ☆
_____	☆ ☆ ☆ ☆ ☆
_____	☆ ☆ ☆ ☆ ☆
_____	☆ ☆ ☆ ☆ ☆

ACCOMPANIST/PERFORMED WITH NOTES

OVERALL THOUGHTS

Ratings ☆ ☆ ☆ ☆ ☆

𝄞 PERFORMANCE LOG

Date _____ Location _____

Accompanist _____ Performed with _____

_____ _____

Songs Performed	Personal Rating
	☆ ☆ ☆ ☆ ☆
	☆ ☆ ☆ ☆ ☆
	☆ ☆ ☆ ☆ ☆
	☆ ☆ ☆ ☆ ☆
	☆ ☆ ☆ ☆ ☆

Accompanist/Performed with Notes

Overall Thoughts

Ratings ☆ ☆ ☆ ☆ ☆

♪ PERFORMANCE LOG

DATE _____ LOCATION _____

ACCOMPANIST _____ PERFORMED WITH _____

_____   _____

SONGS PERFORMED   PERSONAL RATING

	☆ ☆ ☆ ☆ ☆
	☆ ☆ ☆ ☆ ☆
	☆ ☆ ☆ ☆ ☆
	☆ ☆ ☆ ☆ ☆
	☆ ☆ ☆ ☆ ☆

ACCOMPANIST/PERFORMED WITH NOTES

OVERALL THOUGHTS

Ratings ☆ ☆ ☆ ☆ ☆

𝄞 PERFORMANCE LOG

DATE _____ LOCATION _____

ACCOMPANIST _____ PERFORMED WITH _____

_____ _____

SONGS PERFORMED	PERSONAL RATING
	☆ ☆ ☆ ☆ ☆
	☆ ☆ ☆ ☆ ☆
	☆ ☆ ☆ ☆ ☆
	☆ ☆ ☆ ☆ ☆
	☆ ☆ ☆ ☆ ☆

ACCOMPANIST/PERFORMED WITH NOTES

OVERALL THOUGHTS

Ratings ☆ ☆ ☆ ☆ ☆

♪ PERFORMANCE LOG

DATE _____ LOCATION _____

ACCOMPANIST _____ PERFORMED WITH _____

_____   _____

SONGS PERFORMED   PERSONAL RATING

Songs Performed	Personal Rating
_____	☆ ☆ ☆ ☆ ☆
_____	☆ ☆ ☆ ☆ ☆
_____	☆ ☆ ☆ ☆ ☆
_____	☆ ☆ ☆ ☆ ☆
_____	☆ ☆ ☆ ☆ ☆

ACCOMPANIST/PERFORMED WITH NOTES

OVERALL THOUGHTS

Ratings ☆ ☆ ☆ ☆ ☆

♪ PERFORMANCE LOG

DATE _____ LOCATION _____

ACCOMPANIST _____ PERFORMED WITH _____

_____   _____

SONGS PERFORMED   PERSONAL RATING

	☆ ☆ ☆ ☆ ☆
	☆ ☆ ☆ ☆ ☆
	☆ ☆ ☆ ☆ ☆
	☆ ☆ ☆ ☆ ☆
	☆ ☆ ☆ ☆ ☆

ACCOMPANIST/PERFORMED WITH NOTES

OVERALL THOUGHTS

Ratings ☆ ☆ ☆ ☆ ☆

𝄞 PERFORMANCE LOG

DATE _____ LOCATION _____

ACCOMPANIST _____ PERFORMED WITH _____

_____ _____

SONGS PERFORMED

PERSONAL RATING

Songs Performed	Personal Rating
	☆ ☆ ☆ ☆ ☆
	☆ ☆ ☆ ☆ ☆
	☆ ☆ ☆ ☆ ☆
	☆ ☆ ☆ ☆ ☆
	☆ ☆ ☆ ☆ ☆

ACCOMPANIST/PERFORMED WITH NOTES

OVERALL THOUGHTS

Ratings ☆ ☆ ☆ ☆ ☆

𝄞 PERFORMANCE LOG

DATE _____ LOCATION _____

ACCOMPANIST _____ PERFORMED WITH _____

_____ _____

SONGS PERFORMED

Songs Performed	Personal Rating
	☆ ☆ ☆ ☆ ☆
	☆ ☆ ☆ ☆ ☆
	☆ ☆ ☆ ☆ ☆
	☆ ☆ ☆ ☆ ☆
	☆ ☆ ☆ ☆ ☆

ACCOMPANIST/PERFORMED WITH NOTES

OVERALL THOUGHTS

Ratings ☆ ☆ ☆ ☆ ☆

𝄞 PERFORMANCE LOG

DATE _____ LOCATION _____

ACCOMPANIST _____ PERFORMED WITH _____

_____   _____

SONGS PERFORMED   PERSONAL RATING

_____ ☆ ☆ ☆ ☆ ☆

_____ ☆ ☆ ☆ ☆ ☆

_____ ☆ ☆ ☆ ☆ ☆

_____ ☆ ☆ ☆ ☆ ☆

_____ ☆ ☆ ☆ ☆ ☆

ACCOMPANIST/PERFORMED WITH NOTES

OVERALL THOUGHTS

Ratings ☆ ☆ ☆ ☆ ☆

♪ PERFORMANCE LOG

DATE _____ LOCATION _____

ACCOMPANIST _____ PERFORMED WITH _____

_____   _____

SONGS PERFORMED	PERSONAL RATING
	☆ ☆ ☆ ☆ ☆
	☆ ☆ ☆ ☆ ☆
	☆ ☆ ☆ ☆ ☆
	☆ ☆ ☆ ☆ ☆
	☆ ☆ ☆ ☆ ☆

ACCOMPANIST/PERFORMED WITH NOTES

OVERALL THOUGHTS

Ratings ☆ ☆ ☆ ☆ ☆

𝄞 PERFORMANCE LOG

DATE _____ LOCATION _____

ACCOMPANIST _____ PERFORMED WITH _____

_____ _____

SONGS PERFORMED   PERSONAL RATING

_____ ☆ ☆ ☆ ☆ ☆

_____ ☆ ☆ ☆ ☆ ☆

_____ ☆ ☆ ☆ ☆ ☆

_____ ☆ ☆ ☆ ☆ ☆

_____ ☆ ☆ ☆ ☆ ☆

ACCOMPANIST/PERFORMED WITH NOTES

OVERALL THOUGHTS

Ratings ☆ ☆ ☆ ☆ ☆

🎼 PERFORMANCE LOG

DATE _____ LOCATION _____

ACCOMPANIST _____ PERFORMED WITH _____

_____ _____

SONGS PERFORMED   PERSONAL RATING

	☆ ☆ ☆ ☆ ☆
	☆ ☆ ☆ ☆ ☆
	☆ ☆ ☆ ☆ ☆
	☆ ☆ ☆ ☆ ☆
	☆ ☆ ☆ ☆ ☆

ACCOMPANIST/PERFORMED WITH NOTES

OVERALL THOUGHTS

Ratings ☆ ☆ ☆ ☆ ☆

♪ PERFORMANCE LOG

DATE _____ LOCATION _____

ACCOMPANIST _____ PERFORMED WITH _____

_____ _____

SONGS PERFORMED	PERSONAL RATING
_____	☆ ☆ ☆ ☆ ☆
_____	☆ ☆ ☆ ☆ ☆
_____	☆ ☆ ☆ ☆ ☆
_____	☆ ☆ ☆ ☆ ☆
_____	☆ ☆ ☆ ☆ ☆

ACCOMPANIST/PERFORMED WITH NOTES

OVERALL THOUGHTS

Ratings ☆ ☆ ☆ ☆ ☆

♪ PERFORMANCE LOG

DATE _____ LOCATION _____

ACCOMPANIST _____ PERFORMED WITH _____

_____   _____

SONGS PERFORMED   PERSONAL RATING

Songs	Rating
	☆ ☆ ☆ ☆ ☆
	☆ ☆ ☆ ☆ ☆
	☆ ☆ ☆ ☆ ☆
	☆ ☆ ☆ ☆ ☆
	☆ ☆ ☆ ☆ ☆

ACCOMPANIST/PERFORMED WITH NOTES

OVERALL THOUGHTS

Ratings ☆ ☆ ☆ ☆ ☆

♪ PERFORMANCE LOG

DATE _____ LOCATION _____

ACCOMPANIST _____ PERFORMED WITH _____

_____ _____

SONGS PERFORMED

PERSONAL RATING

_____	☆ ☆ ☆ ☆ ☆
_____	☆ ☆ ☆ ☆ ☆
_____	☆ ☆ ☆ ☆ ☆
_____	☆ ☆ ☆ ☆ ☆
_____	☆ ☆ ☆ ☆ ☆

ACCOMPANIST / PERFORMED WITH NOTES

OVERALL THOUGHTS

Ratings ☆ ☆ ☆ ☆ ☆

🎼 PERFORMANCE LOG

DATE _____ LOCATION _____

ACCOMPANIST _____ PERFORMED WITH _____

_____   _____

SONGS PERFORMED | PERSONAL RATING

Songs Performed	Personal Rating
	☆ ☆ ☆ ☆ ☆
	☆ ☆ ☆ ☆ ☆
	☆ ☆ ☆ ☆ ☆
	☆ ☆ ☆ ☆ ☆
	☆ ☆ ☆ ☆ ☆

ACCOMPANIST/PERFORMED WITH NOTES

OVERALL THOUGHTS

Ratings ☆ ☆ ☆ ☆ ☆

𝄞 PERFORMANCE LOG

DATE _____ LOCATION _____

ACCOMPANIST _____ PERFORMED WITH _____

_____   _____

SONGS PERFORMED	PERSONAL RATING
	☆ ☆ ☆ ☆ ☆
	☆ ☆ ☆ ☆ ☆
	☆ ☆ ☆ ☆ ☆
	☆ ☆ ☆ ☆ ☆
	☆ ☆ ☆ ☆ ☆

ACCOMPANIST/PERFORMED WITH NOTES

OVERALL THOUGHTS

Ratings ☆ ☆ ☆ ☆ ☆

𝄞 PERFORMANCE LOG

DATE _____ LOCATION _____

ACCOMPANIST _____ PERFORMED WITH _____

_____ _____

SONGS PERFORMED	PERSONAL RATING
	☆ ☆ ☆ ☆ ☆
	☆ ☆ ☆ ☆ ☆
	☆ ☆ ☆ ☆ ☆
	☆ ☆ ☆ ☆ ☆
	☆ ☆ ☆ ☆ ☆

ACCOMPANIST/PERFORMED WITH NOTES

OVERALL THOUGHTS

Ratings ☆ ☆ ☆ ☆ ☆

🎼 PERFORMANCE LOG

DATE _____ LOCATION _____

ACCOMPANIST _____ PERFORMED WITH _____

_____   _____

SONGS PERFORMED   PERSONAL RATING

	☆ ☆ ☆ ☆ ☆
	☆ ☆ ☆ ☆ ☆
	☆ ☆ ☆ ☆ ☆
	☆ ☆ ☆ ☆ ☆
	☆ ☆ ☆ ☆ ☆

ACCOMPANIST/PERFORMED WITH NOTES

OVERALL THOUGHTS

Ratings ☆ ☆ ☆ ☆ ☆

♪ PERFORMANCE LOG

DATE _____ LOCATION _____

ACCOMPANIST _____ PERFORMED WITH _____

_____ _____

SONGS PERFORMED   PERSONAL RATING

Songs Performed	Personal Rating
	☆ ☆ ☆ ☆ ☆
	☆ ☆ ☆ ☆ ☆
	☆ ☆ ☆ ☆ ☆
	☆ ☆ ☆ ☆ ☆
	☆ ☆ ☆ ☆ ☆

ACCOMPANIST/PERFORMED WITH NOTES

OVERALL THOUGHTS

Ratings ☆ ☆ ☆ ☆ ☆

♪ PERFORMANCE LOG

DATE _____ LOCATION _____

ACCOMPANIST _____ PERFORMED WITH _____

_____   _____

SONGS PERFORMED

		PERSONAL RATING		
☆	☆	☆	☆	☆
☆	☆	☆	☆	☆
☆	☆	☆	☆	☆
☆	☆	☆	☆	☆
☆	☆	☆	☆	☆

ACCOMPANIST/PERFORMED WITH NOTES

OVERALL THOUGHTS

Ratings ☆ ☆ ☆ ☆ ☆

𝄞 PERFORMANCE LOG

DATE _____ LOCATION _____

ACCOMPANIST _____ PERFORMED WITH _____

_____ _____

SONGS PERFORMED   PERSONAL RATING

Songs Performed	Personal Rating
	☆ ☆ ☆ ☆ ☆
	☆ ☆ ☆ ☆ ☆
	☆ ☆ ☆ ☆ ☆
	☆ ☆ ☆ ☆ ☆
	☆ ☆ ☆ ☆ ☆

ACCOMPANIST/PERFORMED WITH NOTES

OVERALL THOUGHTS

Ratings ☆ ☆ ☆ ☆ ☆

𝄞 PERFORMANCE LOG

DATE _____ LOCATION _____

ACCOMPANIST _____ PERFORMED WITH _____

_____ _____

SONGS PERFORMED   PERSONAL RATING

_____	☆ ☆ ☆ ☆ ☆
_____	☆ ☆ ☆ ☆ ☆
_____	☆ ☆ ☆ ☆ ☆
_____	☆ ☆ ☆ ☆ ☆
_____	☆ ☆ ☆ ☆ ☆

ACCOMPANIST/PERFORMED WITH NOTES

OVERALL THOUGHTS

Ratings ☆ ☆ ☆ ☆ ☆

🎼 PERFORMANCE LOG

DATE _____ LOCATION _____

ACCOMPANIST _____ PERFORMED WITH _____

_____ _____

SONGS PERFORMED

	PERSONAL RATING
	☆ ☆ ☆ ☆ ☆
	☆ ☆ ☆ ☆ ☆
	☆ ☆ ☆ ☆ ☆
	☆ ☆ ☆ ☆ ☆
	☆ ☆ ☆ ☆ ☆

ACCOMPANIST/PERFORMED WITH NOTES

OVERALL THOUGHTS

Ratings ☆ ☆ ☆ ☆ ☆

𝄞 PERFORMANCE LOG

DATE _____ LOCATION _____

ACCOMPANIST _____ PERFORMED WITH _____

_____   _____

SONGS PERFORMED

Song		PERSONAL RATING			
	☆	☆	☆	☆	☆
	☆	☆	☆	☆	☆
	☆	☆	☆	☆	☆
	☆	☆	☆	☆	☆
	☆	☆	☆	☆	☆

ACCOMPANIST/PERFORMED WITH NOTES

OVERALL THOUGHTS

Ratings ☆ ☆ ☆ ☆ ☆

♪ PERFORMANCE LOG

DATE _____ LOCATION _____

ACCOMPANIST _____ PERFORMED WITH _____

_____ _____

SONGS PERFORMED   PERSONAL RATING

Songs Performed	Personal Rating
	☆ ☆ ☆ ☆ ☆
	☆ ☆ ☆ ☆ ☆
	☆ ☆ ☆ ☆ ☆
	☆ ☆ ☆ ☆ ☆
	☆ ☆ ☆ ☆ ☆

ACCOMPANIST/PERFORMED WITH NOTES

OVERALL THOUGHTS

Ratings ☆ ☆ ☆ ☆ ☆

𝄞 Performance Log

Date _____ Location _____

Accompanist _____ Performed with _____

_____ _____

Songs Performed

	Personal Rating
_____	☆ ☆ ☆ ☆ ☆
_____	☆ ☆ ☆ ☆ ☆
_____	☆ ☆ ☆ ☆ ☆
_____	☆ ☆ ☆ ☆ ☆
_____	☆ ☆ ☆ ☆ ☆

Accompanist/Performed with Notes

Overall Thoughts

Ratings ☆ ☆ ☆ ☆ ☆

♪ PERFORMANCE LOG

DATE _____ LOCATION _____

ACCOMPANIST _____ PERFORMED WITH _____

_____ _____

SONGS PERFORMED   PERSONAL RATING

Songs	Rating
	☆ ☆ ☆ ☆ ☆
	☆ ☆ ☆ ☆ ☆
	☆ ☆ ☆ ☆ ☆
	☆ ☆ ☆ ☆ ☆
	☆ ☆ ☆ ☆ ☆

ACCOMPANIST/PERFORMED WITH NOTES

OVERALL THOUGHTS

Ratings ☆ ☆ ☆ ☆ ☆

♪ PERFORMANCE LOG

DATE _____ LOCATION _____

ACCOMPANIST _____ PERFORMED WITH _____

_____ _____

SONGS PERFORMED	PERSONAL RATING
	☆ ☆ ☆ ☆ ☆
	☆ ☆ ☆ ☆ ☆
	☆ ☆ ☆ ☆ ☆
	☆ ☆ ☆ ☆ ☆
	☆ ☆ ☆ ☆ ☆

ACCOMPANIST/PERFORMED WITH NOTES

OVERALL THOUGHTS

Ratings ☆ ☆ ☆ ☆ ☆

𝄞 PERFORMANCE LOG

DATE _____ LOCATION _____

ACCOMPANIST _____ PERFORMED WITH _____

_____   _____

SONGS PERFORMED   PERSONAL RATING

Songs Performed	Personal Rating
	☆ ☆ ☆ ☆ ☆
	☆ ☆ ☆ ☆ ☆
	☆ ☆ ☆ ☆ ☆
	☆ ☆ ☆ ☆ ☆
	☆ ☆ ☆ ☆ ☆

ACCOMPANIST/PERFORMED WITH NOTES

OVERALL THOUGHTS

Ratings ☆ ☆ ☆ ☆ ☆

♪ PERFORMANCE LOG

DATE _____ LOCATION _____

ACCOMPANIST _____ PERFORMED WITH _____

_____ _____

SONGS PERFORMED   PERSONAL RATING

_____   ☆ ☆ ☆ ☆ ☆

_____   ☆ ☆ ☆ ☆ ☆

_____   ☆ ☆ ☆ ☆ ☆

_____   ☆ ☆ ☆ ☆ ☆

_____   ☆ ☆ ☆ ☆ ☆

ACCOMPANIST/PERFORMED WITH NOTES

OVERALL THOUGHTS

Ratings ☆ ☆ ☆ ☆ ☆

♪ PERFORMANCE LOG

DATE _____ LOCATION _____

ACCOMPANIST _____ PERFORMED WITH _____

_____   _____

SONGS PERFORMED   PERSONAL RATING

	☆ ☆ ☆ ☆ ☆
	☆ ☆ ☆ ☆ ☆
	☆ ☆ ☆ ☆ ☆
	☆ ☆ ☆ ☆ ☆
	☆ ☆ ☆ ☆ ☆

ACCOMPANIST/PERFORMED WITH NOTES

OVERALL THOUGHTS

Ratings ☆ ☆ ☆ ☆ ☆

𝄞 PERFORMANCE LOG

DATE _____ LOCATION _____

ACCOMPANIST _____ PERFORMED WITH _____

_____ _____

SONGS PERFORMED	PERSONAL RATING
	☆ ☆ ☆ ☆ ☆
	☆ ☆ ☆ ☆ ☆
	☆ ☆ ☆ ☆ ☆
	☆ ☆ ☆ ☆ ☆
	☆ ☆ ☆ ☆ ☆

ACCOMPANIST/PERFORMED WITH NOTES

OVERALL THOUGHTS

Ratings ☆ ☆ ☆ ☆ ☆

♪ PERFORMANCE LOG

DATE _____ LOCATION _____

ACCOMPANIST _____ PERFORMED WITH _____

_____ _____

SONGS PERFORMED

	PERSONAL RATING
	☆ ☆ ☆ ☆ ☆
	☆ ☆ ☆ ☆ ☆
	☆ ☆ ☆ ☆ ☆
	☆ ☆ ☆ ☆ ☆
	☆ ☆ ☆ ☆ ☆

ACCOMPANIST/PERFORMED WITH NOTES

OVERALL THOUGHTS

Ratings ☆ ☆ ☆ ☆ ☆

🎼 PERFORMANCE LOG

DATE _____ LOCATION _____

ACCOMPANIST _____ PERFORMED WITH _____

_____   _____

SONGS PERFORMED   PERSONAL RATING

_____	☆ ☆ ☆ ☆ ☆
_____	☆ ☆ ☆ ☆ ☆
_____	☆ ☆ ☆ ☆ ☆
_____	☆ ☆ ☆ ☆ ☆
_____	☆ ☆ ☆ ☆ ☆

ACCOMPANIST/PERFORMED WITH NOTES

OVERALL THOUGHTS

Ratings   ☆ ☆ ☆ ☆ ☆

♪ PERFORMANCE LOG

DATE _____ LOCATION _____

ACCOMPANIST _____ PERFORMED WITH _____

_____   _____

SONGS PERFORMED   PERSONAL RATING

	☆ ☆ ☆ ☆ ☆
	☆ ☆ ☆ ☆ ☆
	☆ ☆ ☆ ☆ ☆
	☆ ☆ ☆ ☆ ☆
	☆ ☆ ☆ ☆ ☆

ACCOMPANIST/PERFORMED WITH NOTES

OVERALL THOUGHTS

Ratings ☆ ☆ ☆ ☆ ☆

𝄞 PERFORMANCE LOG

DATE _____ LOCATION _____

ACCOMPANIST _____ PERFORMED WITH _____

_____ _____

SONGS PERFORMED | PERSONAL RATING

	☆ ☆ ☆ ☆ ☆
	☆ ☆ ☆ ☆ ☆
	☆ ☆ ☆ ☆ ☆
	☆ ☆ ☆ ☆ ☆
	☆ ☆ ☆ ☆ ☆

ACCOMPANIST/PERFORMED WITH NOTES

OVERALL THOUGHTS

Ratings ☆ ☆ ☆ ☆ ☆

🎼 PERFORMANCE LOG

DATE _____ LOCATION _____

ACCOMPANIST _____ PERFORMED WITH _____

_____ _____

SONGS PERFORMED

	PERSONAL RATING
	☆ ☆ ☆ ☆ ☆
	☆ ☆ ☆ ☆ ☆
	☆ ☆ ☆ ☆ ☆
	☆ ☆ ☆ ☆ ☆
	☆ ☆ ☆ ☆ ☆

ACCOMPANIST/PERFORMED WITH NOTES

OVERALL THOUGHTS

Ratings ☆ ☆ ☆ ☆ ☆

𝄞 PERFORMANCE LOG

DATE _____ LOCATION _____

ACCOMPANIST _____ PERFORMED WITH _____

_____ _____

SONGS PERFORMED

PERSONAL RATING

Song	Rating
_____	☆ ☆ ☆ ☆ ☆
_____	☆ ☆ ☆ ☆ ☆
_____	☆ ☆ ☆ ☆ ☆
_____	☆ ☆ ☆ ☆ ☆
_____	☆ ☆ ☆ ☆ ☆

ACCOMPANIST/PERFORMED WITH NOTES

OVERALL THOUGHTS

Ratings ☆ ☆ ☆ ☆ ☆

♪ PERFORMANCE LOG

DATE _____ LOCATION _____

ACCOMPANIST _____ PERFORMED WITH _____

_____ _____

SONGS PERFORMED   PERSONAL RATING

	☆ ☆ ☆ ☆ ☆
	☆ ☆ ☆ ☆ ☆
	☆ ☆ ☆ ☆ ☆
	☆ ☆ ☆ ☆ ☆
	☆ ☆ ☆ ☆ ☆

ACCOMPANIST/PERFORMED WITH NOTES

OVERALL THOUGHTS

Ratings ☆ ☆ ☆ ☆ ☆

𝄞 PERFORMANCE LOG

DATE _____ LOCATION _____

ACCOMPANIST _____ PERFORMED WITH _____

_____ _____

SONGS PERFORMED	PERSONAL RATING
	☆ ☆ ☆ ☆ ☆
	☆ ☆ ☆ ☆ ☆
	☆ ☆ ☆ ☆ ☆
	☆ ☆ ☆ ☆ ☆
	☆ ☆ ☆ ☆ ☆

ACCOMPANIST/PERFORMED WITH NOTES

OVERALL THOUGHTS

Ratings ☆ ☆ ☆ ☆ ☆

♪ PERFORMANCE LOG

DATE _____ LOCATION _____

ACCOMPANIST _____ PERFORMED WITH _____

_____ _____

SONGS PERFORMED   PERSONAL RATING

	☆ ☆ ☆ ☆ ☆
	☆ ☆ ☆ ☆ ☆
	☆ ☆ ☆ ☆ ☆
	☆ ☆ ☆ ☆ ☆
	☆ ☆ ☆ ☆ ☆

ACCOMPANIST/PERFORMED WITH NOTES

OVERALL THOUGHTS

Ratings ☆ ☆ ☆ ☆ ☆

🎼 PERFORMANCE LOG

DATE _____ LOCATION _____

ACCOMPANIST _____ PERFORMED WITH _____

_____ _____

SONGS PERFORMED   PERSONAL RATING

_____	☆ ☆ ☆ ☆ ☆
_____	☆ ☆ ☆ ☆ ☆
_____	☆ ☆ ☆ ☆ ☆
_____	☆ ☆ ☆ ☆ ☆
_____	☆ ☆ ☆ ☆ ☆

ACCOMPANIST/PERFORMED WITH NOTES

OVERALL THOUGHTS

Ratings ☆ ☆ ☆ ☆ ☆

𝄞 PERFORMANCE LOG

DATE _____ LOCATION _____

ACCOMPANIST _____ PERFORMED WITH _____

_____ _____

SONGS PERFORMED   PERSONAL RATING

	☆ ☆ ☆ ☆ ☆
	☆ ☆ ☆ ☆ ☆
	☆ ☆ ☆ ☆ ☆
	☆ ☆ ☆ ☆ ☆
	☆ ☆ ☆ ☆ ☆

ACCOMPANIST/PERFORMED WITH NOTES

OVERALL THOUGHTS

Ratings ☆ ☆ ☆ ☆ ☆

𝄞 PERFORMANCE LOG

DATE _____ LOCATION _____

ACCOMPANIST _____ PERFORMED WITH _____

_____   _____

SONGS PERFORMED   PERSONAL RATING

	☆ ☆ ☆ ☆ ☆
	☆ ☆ ☆ ☆ ☆
	☆ ☆ ☆ ☆ ☆
	☆ ☆ ☆ ☆ ☆
	☆ ☆ ☆ ☆ ☆

ACCOMPANIST / PERFORMED WITH NOTES

OVERALL THOUGHTS

Ratings ☆ ☆ ☆ ☆ ☆

🎼 PERFORMANCE LOG

DATE _____ LOCATION _____

ACCOMPANIST _____ PERFORMED WITH _____

_____ _____

SONGS PERFORMED | PERSONAL RATING

Songs Performed	Personal Rating
	☆ ☆ ☆ ☆ ☆
	☆ ☆ ☆ ☆ ☆
	☆ ☆ ☆ ☆ ☆
	☆ ☆ ☆ ☆ ☆
	☆ ☆ ☆ ☆ ☆

ACCOMPANIST/PERFORMED WITH NOTES

OVERALL THOUGHTS

Ratings ☆ ☆ ☆ ☆ ☆

♪ PERFORMANCE LOG

DATE _____ LOCATION _____

ACCOMPANIST _____ PERFORMED WITH _____

_____   _____

SONGS PERFORMED

PERSONAL RATING

☆	☆	☆	☆	☆
☆	☆	☆	☆	☆
☆	☆	☆	☆	☆
☆	☆	☆	☆	☆
☆	☆	☆	☆	☆

ACCOMPANIST/PERFORMED WITH NOTES

OVERALL THOUGHTS

Ratings ☆ ☆ ☆ ☆ ☆

♪ PERFORMANCE LOG

DATE _____ LOCATION _____

ACCOMPANIST _____ PERFORMED WITH _____

_____ _____

SONGS PERFORMED	PERSONAL RATING
	☆ ☆ ☆ ☆ ☆
	☆ ☆ ☆ ☆ ☆
	☆ ☆ ☆ ☆ ☆
	☆ ☆ ☆ ☆ ☆
	☆ ☆ ☆ ☆ ☆

ACCOMPANIST/PERFORMED WITH NOTES

OVERALL THOUGHTS

Ratings ☆ ☆ ☆ ☆ ☆

𝄞 PERFORMANCE LOG

DATE _____ LOCATION _____

ACCOMPANIST _____ PERFORMED WITH _____

_____ _____

SONGS PERFORMED

PERSONAL RATING

	☆ ☆ ☆ ☆ ☆
	☆ ☆ ☆ ☆ ☆
	☆ ☆ ☆ ☆ ☆
	☆ ☆ ☆ ☆ ☆
	☆ ☆ ☆ ☆ ☆

ACCOMPANIST/PERFORMED WITH NOTES

OVERALL THOUGHTS

Ratings ☆ ☆ ☆ ☆ ☆

𝄞 PERFORMANCE LOG

DATE _____ LOCATION _____

ACCOMPANIST _____ PERFORMED WITH _____

_____   _____

SONGS PERFORMED	PERSONAL RATING
	☆ ☆ ☆ ☆ ☆
	☆ ☆ ☆ ☆ ☆
	☆ ☆ ☆ ☆ ☆
	☆ ☆ ☆ ☆ ☆
	☆ ☆ ☆ ☆ ☆

ACCOMPANIST/PERFORMED WITH NOTES

OVERALL THOUGHTS

Ratings ☆ ☆ ☆ ☆ ☆

𝄞 PERFORMANCE LOG

DATE _____ LOCATION _____

ACCOMPANIST _____ PERFORMED WITH _____

_____   _____

SONGS PERFORMED   PERSONAL RATING

_____	☆ ☆ ☆ ☆ ☆
_____	☆ ☆ ☆ ☆ ☆
_____	☆ ☆ ☆ ☆ ☆
_____	☆ ☆ ☆ ☆ ☆
_____	☆ ☆ ☆ ☆ ☆

ACCOMPANIST/PERFORMED WITH NOTES

OVERALL THOUGHTS

Ratings ☆ ☆ ☆ ☆ ☆

♪ PERFORMANCE LOG

DATE _____ LOCATION _____

ACCOMPANIST _____ PERFORMED WITH _____

_____ _____

SONGS PERFORMED   PERSONAL RATING

	☆ ☆ ☆ ☆ ☆
	☆ ☆ ☆ ☆ ☆
	☆ ☆ ☆ ☆ ☆
	☆ ☆ ☆ ☆ ☆
	☆ ☆ ☆ ☆ ☆

ACCOMPANIST/PERFORMED WITH NOTES

OVERALL THOUGHTS

Ratings ☆ ☆ ☆ ☆ ☆

♪ PERFORMANCE LOG

DATE _____ LOCATION _____

ACCOMPANIST _____ PERFORMED WITH _____

_____ _____

SONGS PERFORMED

	PERSONAL RATING
	☆ ☆ ☆ ☆ ☆
	☆ ☆ ☆ ☆ ☆
	☆ ☆ ☆ ☆ ☆
	☆ ☆ ☆ ☆ ☆
	☆ ☆ ☆ ☆ ☆

ACCOMPANIST/PERFORMED WITH NOTES

OVERALL THOUGHTS

Ratings ☆ ☆ ☆ ☆ ☆

♪ PERFORMANCE LOG

DATE _____ LOCATION _____

ACCOMPANIST _____ PERFORMED WITH _____

_____   _____

SONGS PERFORMED   PERSONAL RATING

	☆ ☆ ☆ ☆ ☆
	☆ ☆ ☆ ☆ ☆
	☆ ☆ ☆ ☆ ☆
	☆ ☆ ☆ ☆ ☆
	☆ ☆ ☆ ☆ ☆

ACCOMPANIST/PERFORMED WITH NOTES

OVERALL THOUGHTS

Ratings ☆ ☆ ☆ ☆ ☆

🎼 PERFORMANCE LOG

DATE _____ LOCATION _____

ACCOMPANIST _____ PERFORMED WITH _____

_____ _____

SONGS PERFORMED   PERSONAL RATING

_____   ☆ ☆ ☆ ☆ ☆

_____   ☆ ☆ ☆ ☆ ☆

_____   ☆ ☆ ☆ ☆ ☆

_____   ☆ ☆ ☆ ☆ ☆

_____   ☆ ☆ ☆ ☆ ☆

ACCOMPANIST/PERFORMED WITH NOTES

OVERALL THOUGHTS

Ratings ☆ ☆ ☆ ☆ ☆

♪ PERFORMANCE LOG

DATE _____ LOCATION _____

ACCOMPANIST _____ PERFORMED WITH _____

_____   _____

SONGS PERFORMED   PERSONAL RATING

	☆ ☆ ☆ ☆ ☆
	☆ ☆ ☆ ☆ ☆
	☆ ☆ ☆ ☆ ☆
	☆ ☆ ☆ ☆ ☆
	☆ ☆ ☆ ☆ ☆

ACCOMPANIST/PERFORMED WITH NOTES

OVERALL THOUGHTS

Ratings ☆ ☆ ☆ ☆ ☆

𝄞 PERFORMANCE LOG

DATE _____ LOCATION _____

ACCOMPANIST _____ PERFORMED WITH _____

_____ _____

SONGS PERFORMED

	PERSONAL RATING
	☆ ☆ ☆ ☆ ☆
	☆ ☆ ☆ ☆ ☆
	☆ ☆ ☆ ☆ ☆
	☆ ☆ ☆ ☆ ☆
	☆ ☆ ☆ ☆ ☆

ACCOMPANIST/PERFORMED WITH NOTES

OVERALL THOUGHTS

Ratings ☆ ☆ ☆ ☆ ☆

♪ PERFORMANCE LOG

DATE _____ LOCATION _____

ACCOMPANIST _____ PERFORMED WITH _____

_____ _____

SONGS PERFORMED	PERSONAL RATING
	☆ ☆ ☆ ☆ ☆
	☆ ☆ ☆ ☆ ☆
	☆ ☆ ☆ ☆ ☆
	☆ ☆ ☆ ☆ ☆
	☆ ☆ ☆ ☆ ☆

ACCOMPANIST/PERFORMED WITH NOTES

OVERALL THOUGHTS

Ratings ☆ ☆ ☆ ☆ ☆

♪ PERFORMANCE LOG

DATE _____ LOCATION _____

ACCOMPANIST _____ PERFORMED WITH _____

_____ _____

SONGS PERFORMED

PERSONAL RATING

☆	☆	☆	☆	☆
☆	☆	☆	☆	☆
☆	☆	☆	☆	☆
☆	☆	☆	☆	☆
☆	☆	☆	☆	☆

ACCOMPANIST/PERFORMED WITH NOTES

OVERALL THOUGHTS

Ratings ☆ ☆ ☆ ☆ ☆

𝄞 PERFORMANCE LOG

DATE _____ LOCATION _____

ACCOMPANIST _____ PERFORMED WITH _____

_____ _____

SONGS PERFORMED   PERSONAL RATING

Songs Performed	Personal Rating
	☆ ☆ ☆ ☆ ☆
	☆ ☆ ☆ ☆ ☆
	☆ ☆ ☆ ☆ ☆
	☆ ☆ ☆ ☆ ☆
	☆ ☆ ☆ ☆ ☆

ACCOMPANIST/PERFORMED WITH NOTES

OVERALL THOUGHTS

Ratings ☆ ☆ ☆ ☆ ☆

𝄞 PERFORMANCE LOG

DATE _____ LOCATION _____

ACCOMPANIST _____ PERFORMED WITH _____

_____   _____

SONGS PERFORMED   PERSONAL RATING

	☆ ☆ ☆ ☆ ☆
	☆ ☆ ☆ ☆ ☆
	☆ ☆ ☆ ☆ ☆
	☆ ☆ ☆ ☆ ☆
	☆ ☆ ☆ ☆ ☆

ACCOMPANIST/PERFORMED WITH NOTES

OVERALL THOUGHTS

Ratings ☆ ☆ ☆ ☆ ☆

𝄞 PERFORMANCE LOG

DATE _____ LOCATION _____

ACCOMPANIST _____ PERFORMED WITH _____

_____ _____

SONGS PERFORMED

Songs Performed	Personal Rating
	☆ ☆ ☆ ☆ ☆
	☆ ☆ ☆ ☆ ☆
	☆ ☆ ☆ ☆ ☆
	☆ ☆ ☆ ☆ ☆
	☆ ☆ ☆ ☆ ☆

ACCOMPANIST/PERFORMED WITH NOTES

OVERALL THOUGHTS

Ratings ☆ ☆ ☆ ☆ ☆

𝄞 PERFORMANCE LOG

DATE _____ LOCATION _____

ACCOMPANIST _____ PERFORMED WITH _____

_____   _____

SONGS PERFORMED   PERSONAL RATING

Songs	☆	☆	☆	☆	☆
	☆	☆	☆	☆	☆
	☆	☆	☆	☆	☆
	☆	☆	☆	☆	☆
	☆	☆	☆	☆	☆

ACCOMPANIST/PERFORMED WITH NOTES

OVERALL THOUGHTS

Ratings ☆ ☆ ☆ ☆ ☆

Made in the USA
Las Vegas, NV
12 December 2021

37207026R00057